Pet Expert

CATS

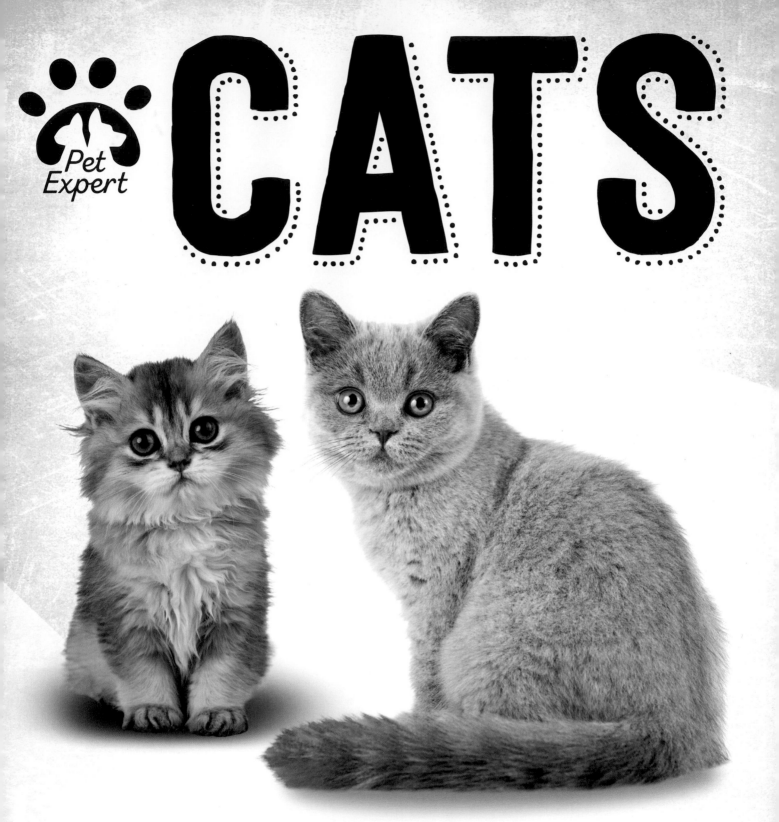

By Gemma Barder

WAYLAND

www.waylandbooks.co.uk

PET EXPERT: CATS!

Cats are one of the world's best-loved pets, but how much do you know about these fabulous felines? This book is crammed with everything you need to know to become a Pet Expert on cats, from rare breeds to famous felines and everything in between. Plus there are top tips on how to look after your kitten and help it to grow up happy and healthy.

CONTENTS

UNFAMILIAR FELINES

KITTENS

MILLIONS OF MOGGIES

Did you know that there are 58 recognised breeds of domestic cat in the world? Time to get to know some of the most popular ones!

THE DOMESTIC SHORTHAIR

The world's most-popular cat has a mixed ancestry and doesn't sit within the British and American Shorthair pedigree breeds. It's sometimes called a 'house cat' or a 'moggie'. They have short hair and can be a variety of colours with patches of white and black.

FACTFILE

It's official, owning a cat is good for your health!

■ Stroking a cat reduces stress levels, which keeps your heart healthy.

■ In a survey, 41 per cent of cat owners said they slept better with a cat in their bedroom.

■ Having a pet you love releases a chemical in your brain called oxytocin. This clever chemical not only makes you feel happy, it can also be good for your digestion.

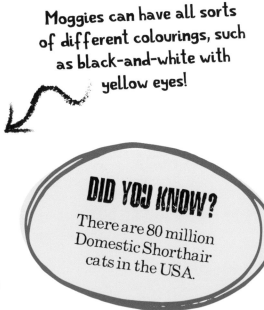

Moggies can have all sorts of different colourings, such as black-and-white with yellow eyes!

DID YOU KNOW?

There are 80 million Domestic Shorthair cats in the USA.

BRITISH SHORTHAIR

This cat is the pedigree version of a Domestic Shorthair. It has amber eyes and a thick, short coat, which is usually a blue-grey colour. British Shorthairs are good-natured, easy to groom and don't have many health problems – which makes them the perfect pet!

MAINE COON

The Maine Coon is one of the largest domestic cats as it can grow to around 1 metre long and weigh between 3-5 kg. It has a long, fluffy coat and a big bushy tail and was used as a farm cat thanks to its fantastic ability to hunt mice. They are now very popular (and very stylish!) pets.

PERSIAN

With its short, compact face and little snub nose, the Persian cat is very recognisable. Their coats need brushing daily, so they need a bit more looking after than a shorthair, but they are very affectionate and love to be stroked.

This gorgeous kitty needs lots of pampering and attention – but she deserves it!

DID YOU KNOW?

A Maine Coon cat had a starring role in the *Harry Potter* films! She played caretaker Argus Filch's cat, Mrs Norris.

UNFAMILIAR FELINES

Sacred kitties and cats with no fur; read all about these lesser-known breeds.

This strong and sturdy cat is actually a big softie on the inside.

PETERBALD

As the name suggests, these kitties are completely furless – although they are sometimes born with soft down that disappears as they grow. Despite looking a little different to a regular cat, Peterbalds are very loving and affectionate.

KURILIAN BOBTAIL

Kurilian Bobtails are stocky, fluffy and very clever. In their native Kuril Islands (near Japan and Russia) they are known as great hunters, but are very gentle with their owners. They get their name thanks to their short tail. One of the reasons they are so rare is that Kurilian Bobtails only have two or three kittens in a litter.

EGYPTIAN MAU

These regal looking cats are one of the only spotted domestic cat breeds in the world. They are also super speedy! They were worshipped in ancient Egypt as a sacred animal and their image can be found on statues, carvings, and inside Pharaohs' tombs.

FACT FILE

Some of the most recognisable big cats are also some of the most endangered.

■ Tigers: the Malayan Tiger is the most endangered tiger on the planet. There are thought to only be 250-340 left in the world. Their biggest threat comes from the loss of their natural habitat in Malaysia and from poaching.

■ Lions: although not as endangered as some tigers, the African Lion has recently been classed as vulnerable and its population is decreasing. There are about 20,000 lions left in the wild.

77 kph

48 kph

An Egyptian Mau can run up to 77 kph, while many other domestic cats can only run around 48 kph.

CAT CHAT

Do you know what it means when your cat purrs or what your cat's tail is trying to tell you? Time to find out if you are right!

TAIL

Although cats use their tails mainly for balance, tails also reveal clues about your cat's mood. A tail in the air with the tip pointed towards you is a friendly greeting. A swaying, halfway-down tail means your cat is confused or trying to make a decision.

FACT FILE

Cats rub the sides of their heads and bodies against people and objects for several reasons:

- to say 'hello'
- to spread their scent and mark their territory
- to pick up scent information from animals or other cats.

EARS

A cat's ears are surprisingly flexible and they can tell you a lot about how your cat is feeling. Soft or rounded ears mean your cat is relaxed. Pointed straight up means your cat is alert to something around them, and flat back or to the side means that they are anxious or frightened.

TUMMY

When a cat rolls over and shows you its tummy, they are saying hello and showing you they are happy. Unlike dogs, cats don't usually want their tummies rubbed and would prefer a quick nose scratch instead!

DID YOU KNOW?

Cats don't just purr when they are happy, they can also purr to keep themselves calm, which is why they often purr at the vets, or even before they have kittens!

EYES

If a cat slowly blinks their eyes at you, it's a good sign. The slow blink means that the cat trusts you and isn't afraid. When you meet a new cat, try doing a slow blink at them to show them you are just as chilled out.

KITTENS

There's no doubt that kittens are some of the cutest baby animals, but they also need lots of special care and attention.

CHOOSING YOUR KITTEN

Before you bring a kitten into your home, make sure you pick the right one. Remember that longhair breeds need plenty of grooming. Talk to the owners of the kitten and ask to meet its parents, too, to see what sort of cat it might grow into.

DID YOU KNOW?
Kittens can sleep for up to 18 hours a day!

BRINGING THEM HOME

Your kitten will find their new home a little strange at first, so you will need to be very calm and patient when they first arrive. Put their bed in a quiet cosy spot and let them explore at their own pace.

ON THE TABLE

Your kitten may not eat much
when they first arrive, but they'll soon
be gobbling up whatever you put
out for them. Kittens can eat wet
or dry food, but try to get special
kitten food that contains lots
of the vitamins they need.

FACT FILE

■ Kittens are born in litters
of between one and nine.

■ They can't see clearly
or hear very well until they are
three weeks old.

■ Kittens become cats
when they are between six
months and a year old.

■ The word kitten means
'little cat' in old French.

KITTY CARE

From feeding to grooming, learn everything you need to know to keep your kitty happy.

PURR-FECT GROOMING

Cats do a great job of keeping themselves clean. However, there are still plenty of things for you to help with. Brush your cat at least once a week to get rid of any dead skin and matted fur and check your cat's eyes and ears for signs of infection.

FOOD AND DRINK

Like most animals, cats need a fresh, clean supply of water on hand at all times (especially in warm weather). Choose a cat food that contains taurine (a type of amino acid) as this is great for their heart and eyes.

KITTY LITTER

When cats are indoors they like to use a litter tray. Make sure you keep it in the same spot so that your cat knows where to find it. Clean out any soiled litter as soon as you spot it. Cats can be quite fussy and might not use a dirty litter tray!

PAW PATROL

Cats love exploring, so from time to time they may get things like pebbles, dirt or even small toys stuck in their paws. Keep an eye on how your cat is walking and check their paws for signs of sores.

DID YOU KNOW?

Despite cats often being thought of as loving cream and milk, a lot of cats can't digest dairy.

DANGEROUS PLANTS

Although most cats are particular about their food, you may need to be careful about some plants that come into your home if you have a cat. Lilies are particularly poisonous to cats and their pollen can be accidentally knocked into food. If you have a cat that likes to nibble grass, try growing cat-friendly plants, such as catnip and mint.

FLEA AND WORM TREATMENT

Fleas and worms can be picked up very easily by your cat (especially if they are an outdoor cat). An adult cat should have a flea and worm treatment every three months. Treatments can be as simple as placing a cream on your cat's back, to mixing in some medicine with their food.

MICROCHIPPING

Microchipping is a small painless procedure that places a tiny microchip (about the size of a grain of rice) under your cat's skin. If your cat ever gets lost, the microchip can be scanned to reveal who they belong to.

Spend quality time with your cat by playing with balls, toy mice and bits of ribbon and string.

FACT FILE

BATH TIME

Cats tend to hate getting wet, but if your cat *really* needs a bath:

- Choose a time when your cat is relaxed.
- Place a rubber bath mat in the bottom of the bath to stop them from slipping.
- Use pet shampoo to avoid drying out your cat's skin.
- Place a little cotton wool ball in each ear.
- Wrap them in a large warm towel at the end.

THE RIGHT CATTITUDE

Here are our top tips for looking after your cat. Make sure you have everything covered before bringing home your fluffy bundle.

DO:

✔ check if any family members are allergic to cats before you bring one home.

✔ keep any top floor windows closed or on a latch to prevent curious kitties from getting stuck!

✔ play with cat toys! Cats love to chase and pounce, so get your kitty a little toy mouse or feathers on a string.

✔ give your cat space when they are eating in case you make them nervous.

Outdoors or indoors? Some cat breeds need to be kept indoors, while others are happier if they can wander outdoors where they like. Ask your vet if you are unsure.

DON'T:

✗

feed your cat too much. Overweight moggies can develop health problems, such as arthritis and diabetes.

✗

stroke their tail. Cats love their backs, ears and chin being scratched, but aren't so keen on people touching their tails.

✗

be negative. Cats don't respond well to shouting or telling off and you might lose your bond.

✗

skip flea treatments. Cats can pick up fleas easily, especially if they are outdoor cats.

✓ # FOOD FOR CATS ✗

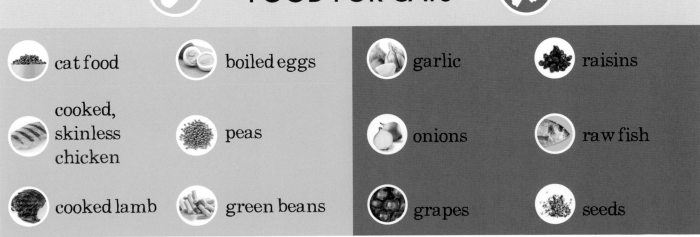

✓		✗	
cat food	boiled eggs	garlic	raisins
cooked, skinless chicken	peas	onions	raw fish
cooked lamb	green beans	grapes	seeds

CAT COMFORT

Time to learn how to give your cat the best home and show them just how much you love them.

A bed with a hood can be a great idea for a new cat as it will give them somewhere to snuggle up and feel safe!

HOME FROM HOME

No matter how far your cat roams during the day, they'll always need a safe cosy spot to come home to. Give your cat their own bed with a soft warm cushion to snuggle up on. Wash the bedding at least once a week.

SLOW AND STEADY

When you are moving house or bringing home a new cat, take things slowly. Introduce your cat to one room at a time and let them decide where they want to explore next. Cats can be nervous in new surroundings, so give them lots of reassurance.

SCRATCHING IS GOOD!

Cats need to scratch. It helps them to file down their claws and keep them healthy. A scratching post can be a great way of keeping your furniture free of claw marks.

DID YOU KNOW?

Cats can sleep for up to 17 hours a day. They are crepuscular, which means they are most awake at dawn and dusk.

FACT FILE

Why do cats scratch? You might get annoyed at your cat for scratching your bedposts or the corner of your favourite chair, but scratching is very important for your kitty. Here's why:

- it keeps their claws fresh
- it marks their territory
- it spreads their scent
- it helps them stretch.

POUNCE THROUGH THE PAST

Cats have been worshipped, given royal protection and become Internet stars. Find out about their incredible history!

CHINA

About 2,500 years ago the ancient Egyptians gave a cat to the Emperor of China. Cats soon became a status symbol of the Song Dynasty. Later, Egyptian cats were bred with Chinese wildcats, which resulted in new breeds, such as Siamese and Burmese.

2000 BCE
500 BCE
CE 900s

EGYPT

The first record of cats living with humans can be found almost 4,000 years ago in ancient Egypt. They were kept to stop crops from being destroyed by mice and rats. They were so good at their job that lots of food could be grown.

EUROPE

Cats soon became known for their vermin-busting skills. In the 10th century, the king of Wales, Hywel Dda (880–950), gave cats official royal protection. This meant that anyone who killed a cat could be sentenced to death!

DID YOU KNOW?

Thanks to their superhero-style efforts, cats became sacred creatures in ancient Egypt and were often associated with the goddess Bastet.

2 million

25 billion

There are over 2 million cat videos on YouTube and they have been watched 25 billion times!

A ROYAL REUNION

Cats became popular as family pets. When Queen Victoria (1819–1901) added a cat to her household, cats became uber-fashionable.

CE 1300s	1800s	1990s

WITCHCRAFT

In the Middle Ages, cats became associated with witches and witchcraft, so by the middle of the 14th century they had become less popular. Because of this, rodent populations grew, which meant rodent-infested homes, towns and cities were much more common.

A POPULAR PET

In the 1990s cats officially took over from dogs as the world's most-popular pet! Their popularity can be seen everywhere, from books and films to the Internet, where you can watch millions of videos and memes of people's beloved cats.

FAMOUS FELINES

Ever heard of the 'unsinkable' cat? Or the kitty that's met some of the most important people in the world? Read on to discover more.

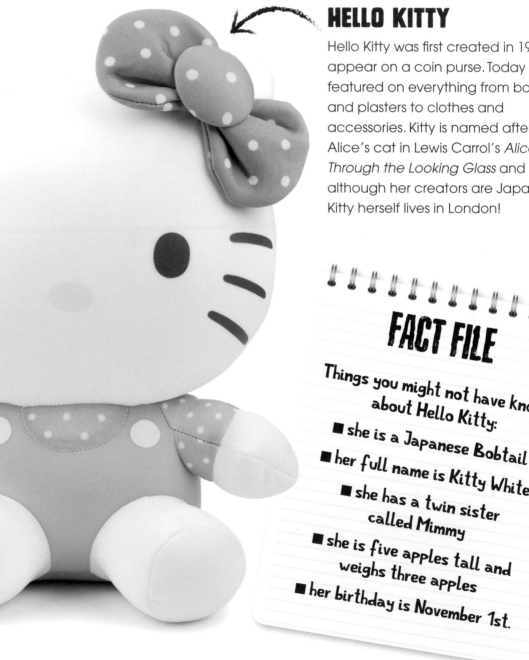

HELLO KITTY

Hello Kitty was first created in 1974 to appear on a coin purse. Today she is featured on everything from books and plasters to clothes and accessories. Kitty is named after Alice's cat in Lewis Carrol's *Alice Through the Looking Glass* and although her creators are Japanese, Kitty herself lives in London!

FACT FILE

Things you might not have known about Hello Kitty:

- she is a Japanese Bobtail
- her full name is Kitty White
- she has a twin sister called Mimmy
- she is five apples tall and weighs three apples
- her birthday is November 1st.

LARRY THE DOWNING STREET CAT

There have been many 'chief mousers' at Downing Street (the Prime Minister of Great Britain's official residence) over the years, including Larry. This cat has met some important people, including former US president Barack Obama (1961–). But he can be a little grumpy with other cats (he prefers VIPs!).

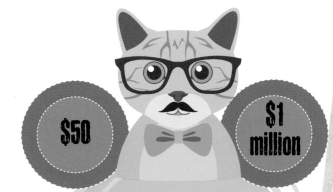

$50

$1 million

The average cat costs $50 dollars in the USA. Grumpy Cat is thought to be worth $1,000,000!

UNSINKABLE SAM

Sam was a very lucky cat who lived on board both German and British ships during the Second World War (1939–45). He survived not one, but three shipwrecks before being taken back to England to live the rest of his life in a home for sailors.

HMS *Ark Royal* aircraft carrier after being torpedoed in 1941

GRUMPY CAT

Grumpy Cat became an Internet sensation in 2012 when her owner's brother posted a picture of her on social media. She soon became a star with posters, books and T-shirts made of her adorable face. Her real name is Tardar Sauce and she has a feline version of dwarfism.

CLAWSOME CATS

Oldest, longest, smallest? They're all here in these pages of feline record breakers!

Ligers can only be seen in zoos and nature reserves.

OLD-TIMER

Creme Puff was born in 1967 in Austin, Texas, USA, and lived for 38 years and three days – that's double the average life expectancy for a cat. Creme Puff's owner believed it was down to the unusual food he fed her, including bacon and broccoli.

ONE LOUD PURR

The loudest purr ever recorded by the *Guinness Book of Records* was by a cat called Merlin from Torquay in England. He was recorded at 67.8 decibels, which is as loud as a car going 104 kph!

DID YOU KNOW?

The biggest cat in the world is a Liger (a cross between a lion and a tigress) called Hercules who stands at 3.33 m tall!

TEENY TINY KITTY

A Blue Point Himalayan-Persian cat called Tinker Toy is the world's smallest cat to date. He was only 7 cm tall and 19 cm long when he was fully grown!

Tinker Toy was a Himalyan-Persian, like this one!

BEST BY A WHISKER

Missi, a Maine Coon cat from Finland, officially has the longest whiskers of any domestic cat in the world. Her fabulous feelers measured 19 cm long!

BIG AND BEAUTIFUL

Maine Coon cats certainly like to show off when it comes to being the biggest. Stewie was measured as being 1.23 m long in 2010 in Reno, Nevada, USA. He still holds the record for being the longest cat ever.

Maine **Coon** cats are large, fluffy and beautiful - just like this kitty!

FIVE FACTS

Ever wondered why your kitten is so sleepy, or who invented the cat flap? Get ready to discover five things you never knew about cats.

1 CATS CAN'T TASTE SWEET THINGS

The tiny cells inside a cat's taste buds are formed differently to other animals, which means they can't taste sugar.

2 A CAT'S NOSE IS UNIQUE

The bumps on a cat's nose are similar to a human's fingerprint. No two cats have the same nose print.

3 SIR ISAAC NEWTON MADE LIFE EASIER FOR CATS

The famous physicist and mathematician actually invented the cat flap. According to history, Sir Isaac's cat kept opening the door to his laboratory while he was conducting experiments with light. To solve this, he invented a small door that would allow his cat to move between rooms without opening the door and letting too much light in.

SIR ISAAC NEWTON (1642-1727)

4 CATS CAN BE RIGHT- OR LEFT-PAWED

Just like humans, cats like to use either their right or left paw for simple tasks. What's even more interesting is that most male cats are left-pawed and most female cats are right-pawed!

5 KITTENS GROW IN THEIR SLEEP

What a clever trick! Kittens only produce the special hormone they need to grow when they are fast asleep. So that's why kittens spend most of their time snoozing!

THE COOLEST CAT

Find out what type of cat would be your perfect feline match.

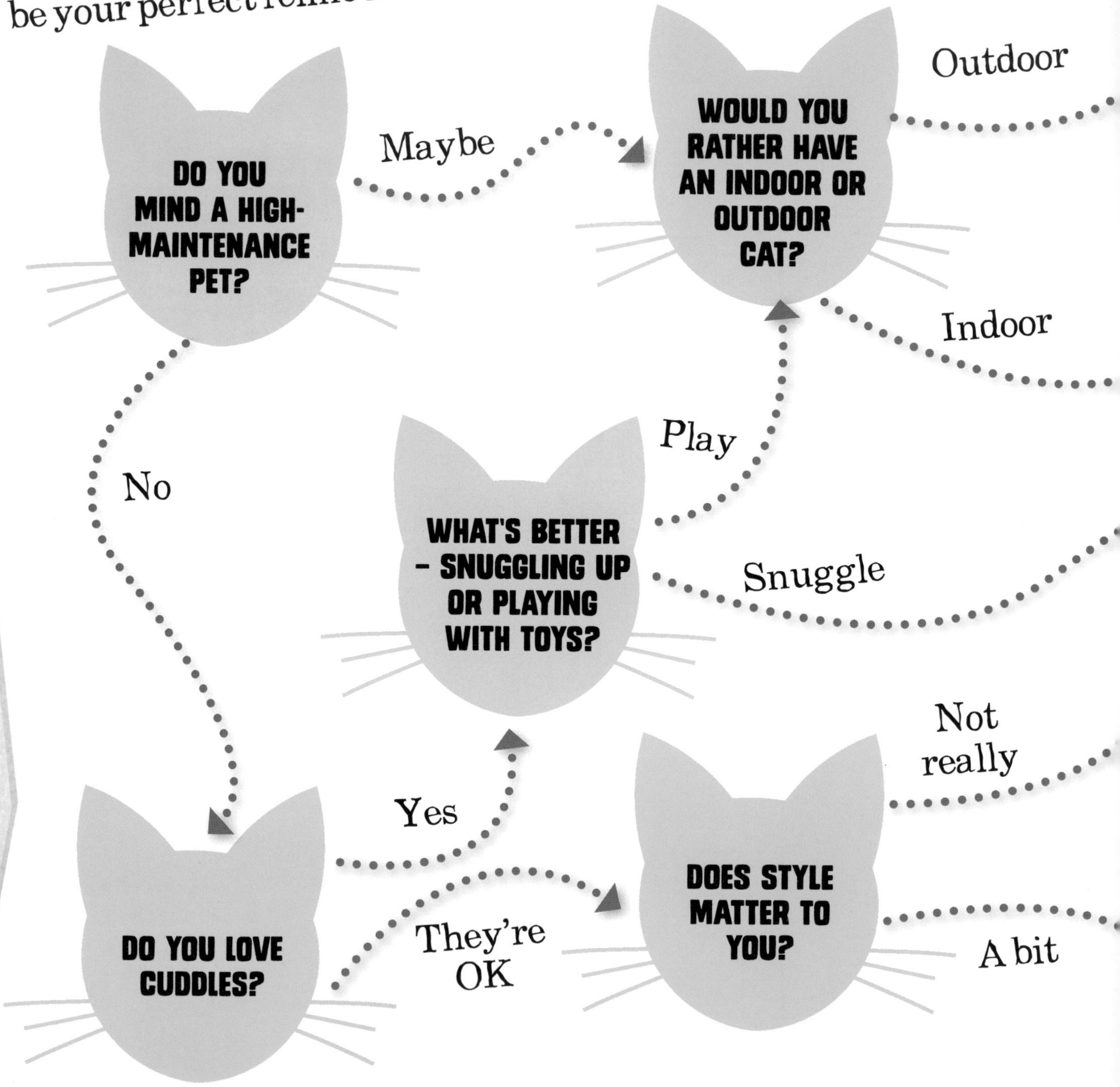

DO YOU MIND A HIGH-MAINTENANCE PET?

Maybe

WOULD YOU RATHER HAVE AN INDOOR OR OUTDOOR CAT?

Outdoor

Indoor

No

WHAT'S BETTER – SNUGGLING UP OR PLAYING WITH TOYS?

Play

Snuggle

Not really

Yes

DO YOU LOVE CUDDLES?

They're OK

DOES STYLE MATTER TO YOU?

A bit

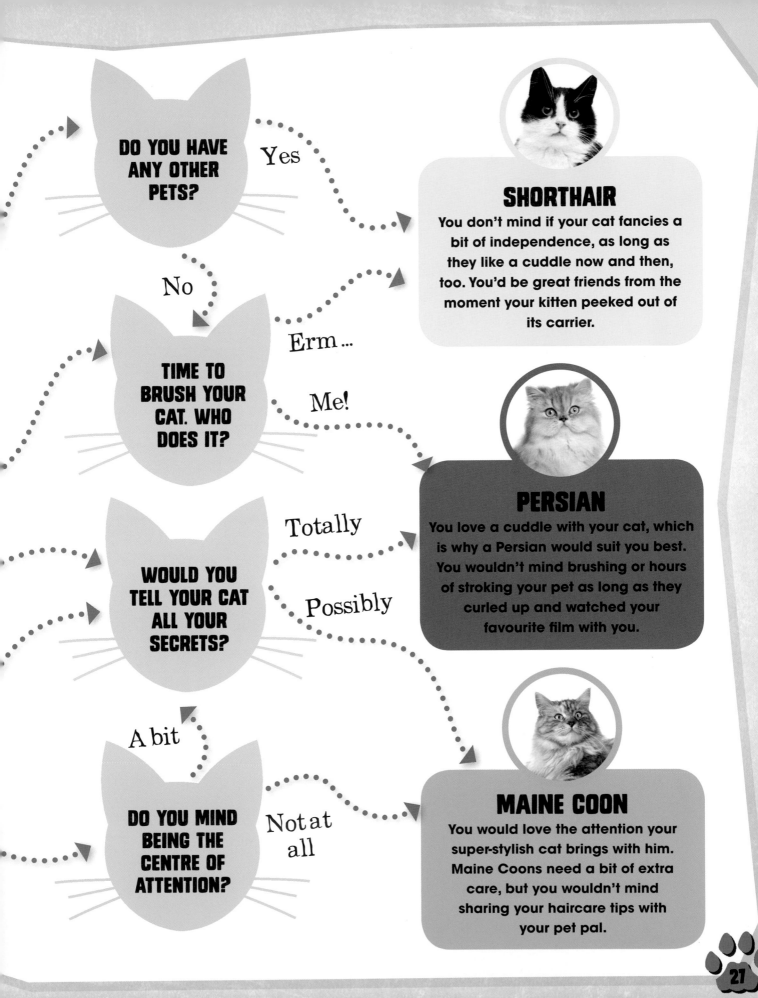

DO YOU HAVE ANY OTHER PETS?

Yes

No

Erm...

Me!

TIME TO BRUSH YOUR CAT. WHO DOES IT?

WOULD YOU TELL YOUR CAT ALL YOUR SECRETS?

Totally

Possibly

A bit

DO YOU MIND BEING THE CENTRE OF ATTENTION?

Not at all

SHORTHAIR

You don't mind if your cat fancies a bit of independence, as long as they like a cuddle now and then, too. You'd be great friends from the moment your kitten peeked out of its carrier.

PERSIAN

You love a cuddle with your cat, which is why a Persian would suit you best. You wouldn't mind brushing or hours of stroking your pet as long as they curled up and watched your favourite film with you.

MAINE COON

You would love the attention your super-stylish cat brings with him. Maine Coons need a bit of extra care, but you wouldn't mind sharing your haircare tips with your pet pal.

QUIZ!

It's time to test everything you have learned in your book! Are you the pet expert on cats?

1 IN WHAT FILM DOES A MAINE COON HAVE A STARRING ROLE AS THE CARETAKER'S CAT?

a) *Nanny McPhee*
b) *Harry Potter*
c) *A Series of Unfortunate Events*

2 WHAT IS THE NAME OF A FURLESS CAT BREED?

a) Peterbald
b) Johnbald
c) Alanbald

3 WHAT SHOULD YOU DO WHEN A CAT ROLLS ON ITS BACK?

a) scratch its tummy
b) ignore them
c) say hello and stroke their nose

4 WHAT DOES THE WORD 'KITTEN' MEAN IN OLD FRENCH?

a) small cat
b) cute
c) big paws

5 WHERE SHOULD YOU AVOID STROKING A CAT?

a) tail
b) back
c) ears

Turn over to read the answers and discover if you are a pet expert!

6 WHY DO CATS NEED TO SCRATCH?

a) to keep their claws healthy?
b) to spread their scent?
c) both of the above

7 WHY WERE CATS SO POPULAR IN ANCIENT EGYPT?

a) because they helped to build the pyramids
b) because they killed vermin and helped crops grow
c) because they were the Pharaohs' favourite animal

8 HOW MANY CATS ARE THOUGHT TO BE ALIVE IN THE WORLD?

a) 60 million
b) 600 million
c) 6 million

9 WHAT IS HELLO KITTY'S FULL NAME?

a) Kitty Brown
b) Kitty Cat
c) Kitty White

10 WHAT TYPE OF CAT HOLDS THE WORLD RECORD FOR THE LONGEST WHISKERS?

a) Persian
b) British Shorthair
c) Maine Coon

GLOSSARY

ALLERGIC
To have an allergy to something. Some people cough, sneeze and have itchy eyes when they are near cat fur.

ANXIOUS
Feeling worried or nervous about something

ARTHRITIS
A disease that causes pain and stiffness in your joints

BREED
A group of the same animal that share the same appearance and characteristics

DIABETES
A disease where the body cannot respond properly to the hormone, insulin, which causes raised levels of glucose (sugar) in the blood

DOMESTIC
A domestic cat is one that lives with humans

ENDANGERED
At risk of extinction (meaning that there will be none of that kind left in the world)

GROOMING
To brush your cat, clean them and trim their nails

LITTER
The name given to a group of kittens born at the same time to the same mother

LITTER TRAY
The place a cat goes to the toilet when they are inside

MEME
A funny video or image that is shared on the Internet

PEDIGREE
A pure-bred cat

POACHING
To illegally hunt or catch animals

PURR
The vibrating sound a cat makes

STATUS SYMBOL
Something that shows off how much money you have

VERMIN
Wild animals that cause problems, such as eating crops or damaging property

QUIZ ANSWERS

1. B.   2. A.   3. C.   4. A.   5. A.   6. C.   7. B.   8. B.   9. C.   10. C.

INDEX

First published in Great Britain in 2019 by Wayland

Copyright © Hodder and Stoughton, 2019

All rights reserved

Editor: Dynamo Limited

Designer: Dynamo Limited

HB ISBN: 978 1 5263 0861 0

PB ISBN: 978 1 5263 0862 7

Printed and bound in China

Wayland, an imprint of

Hachette Children's Group

Part of Hodder and Stoughton

Carmelite House

50 Victoria Embankment

London EC4Y 0DZ

An Hachette UK Company

www.hachette.co.uk

www.hachettechildrens.co.uk

FSC
www.fsc.org

MIX
Paper from
responsible sources
FSC® C104740

The website addresses (URLs) included in this book were valid at the time of going to press. However, it is possible that contents or addresses may have changed since the publication of this book. No responsibility for any such changes can be accepted by either the author or the Publisher.

Picture acknowledgements:

All images courtesy of Getty Images iStock apart from:
Cat'chy Images/Shutterstock: front cover l, Everett Collection/Alamy:21br, Pictorial Press Ltd/Alamy: 21c, Tierfotoagentur/Alamy: 23tr.
(Key: l - left, br - bottom right, c - centre, tr - top right)

Every attempt has been made to clear copyright. Should there be any inadvertent omission please apply to the publisher for rectification.